Kitchen Maths

sex

About Starters Maths books

STARTERS MATHS have been designed to highlight for young children some everyday situations, to which New Mathematics apply. The topic approach has been used to help the children relate mathematics to the ordinary world around them, by presenting money, number, shape, size and other mathematical ideas in familiar contexts. Children will be able to consolidate their experience in arranging sets, in recognising simple geometric forms and in using other mathematical ideas in ways now widely practised by their teachers. The books also follow the normal school practice of using only metric measures.

The text of each book is simple enough to enable children to read the questions for themselves, as the vocabulary has been carefully controlled to ensure that about 90% of the words used will be familiar to them.

Illustrated by: Dennis Evans

Written and planned by: Leslie Foster, former Primary School Headmaster and Inspector for Schools, author of *Colour Factor in Action, Play's the Thing, Classes and Counts, Countdown to Christmas, Countdown to Easter* and *Just Look At Computers.*

Managing editor: Su Swallow

Editor: Sandie Oram

Production: Rosemary Bishop

Chairman, teacher panel: F. F. Blackwell, former General Inspector for Schools, London Borough of Croydon, with responsibility for Primary Education.

Teacher panel: Ruth Lucas, Linda Snowden, Mary Todd

ISBN 0 356 04428 9
(cased edition)

ISBN 0 356 11095 8
(limp edition)

© Macdonald and Company (Publishers) Limited 1973
Reprinted 1974 and 1984
Made and printed in Great Britain by Hazell, Watson & Viney Limited Aylesbury, Buckinghamshire

First published in 1973 by Macdonald and Company (Publishers) Limited
Maxwell House
Worship Street
London EC2A 2EN

Members of BPCC plc

STARTERS MATHS

Kitchen Maths

Macdonald Educational

This girl is in the kitchen.
She is laying the table for tea.
How many spoons has she put out?
How many forks will she need?
2

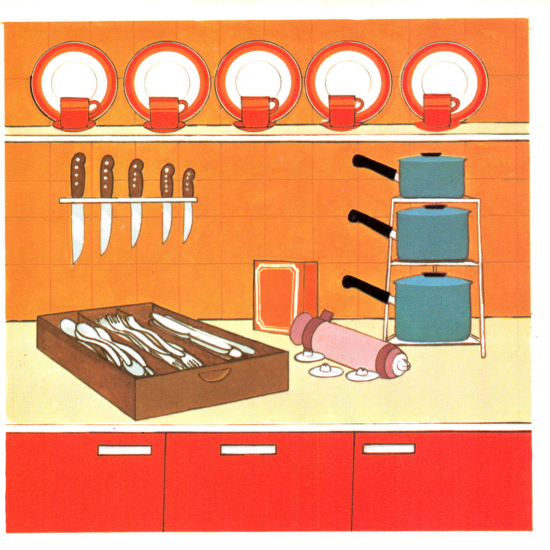

There are many sets in the kitchen.
Can you see a set of knives?
What other sets can you see?
Which set has the least things in it?

3

Count the blue saucepans in the picture.
Find the small red saucepans.
Look at the saucepans in the rack.
Are they in any order?

4

Everything in the kitchen takes up space.
Some of the things are shaped like boxes.
Look at each face of a box.
Do you know what shape they are?

Look at the shapes in the kitchen.
Can you see the rectangles?
Squares are a kind of rectangle.
Can you find the squares?

6

These children are filling a bowl
with water.
They are using mugs to fill it.
How many mugs will fill your bowl?

7

Pour a jugful of water into a jar.
Then pour it into a bigger jar.
Is the amount of water the same?
Try this with some other jars.

8

Some machines measure mass.
What is the mass of a packet of sugar?
Try weighing things on a spring balance.

9

Get two boxes of the same size.
Fill one with macaroni
and one with sugar.
Find out which is heavier.

10

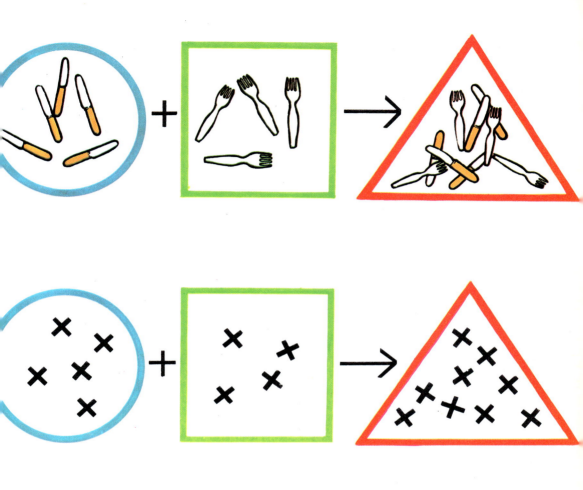

Here are sets of knives and forks.
Count the knives and then the forks.
Add the number of knives
to the number of forks.

11

Mother is ironing a handkerchief.
It covers part of the table.
The towel covers part of the wall.
Which of them covers more space?

12

Make some dough.
Cover a plate with dough.
Cut out some shapes from the dough.
Make some long and some short shapes.

Clocks tell us the time.
When you bake a cake
you need a timer.
What does it do?
14

Point to $\frac{1}{2}$ past an hour on a clock.
Measure $\frac{1}{2}$ a litre of water.
Can you pour $\frac{1}{2}$ a glass of water?
Find something with a mass of $\frac{1}{2}$ kilogram.

15

There are many wheels in the kitchen.
The pastry wheel rolls along.
The whisk rotates.
What else do you think rotates?

16

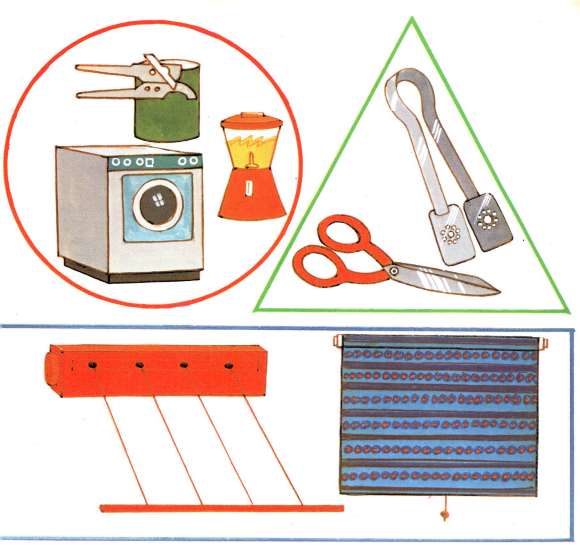

Here are some kitchen sets.
The blind is a kind of pulley.
What else is in the set of pulleys?
Do you know how the other sets work?

17

Here is a set of crockery.
It is sorted into sub-sets.
What is in each sub-set?
Why is the spoon outside the set?
18

Here is a graph of the crockery.
Which set has the least?
Are there more plates than cups?
Can you make a graph of your cutlery?

Look at the lines in the picture.
Most of these lines are straight.
What shapes do the lines
which cross make?

20

Look at all these curved shapes.
Can you find the cylinders?

Here are some different shapes.
Can you find the rectangles?
Find the square rectangles.
Can you see the set of triangles?
22

Tiles cover the kitchen walls and floor.
They make a pattern.
The blind has a pattern too.
Can you make patterns like these?

It is hot in the kitchen.
How do we know how hot the oven is?
How can we measure the temperature?
What is the temperature today?

24

One boy measures his height on the door.
He can see how he has grown.
Try growing some bulbs.
Mark how much they grow each week.

more than 1 litre

1 litre

less than 1 litre

Collect some jars.
Find those which hold a litre.
How many hold more than a litre?
How many hold less?

Find a bottle which holds a litre.
Can you measure $\frac{1}{2}$ a litre of water?
How much water fills the other bottles?

27

Index

Notes for Parents and Teachers

Here is a brief explanation of the various mathematical points covered in this book, to help the interested adult to explore the topic with children.

Sets and numbers *(pages 2, 3, 4, 11, 18)*

Sets are one of the starting points of modern mathematics. Children sort things into sets and put them in order of size, colour or type *(4, 18)*. They experience counting by matching an object in one set to a thing or person in another set *(2)*. Through various opportunities for counting with sets, they can develop an understanding of the processes involved in addition and subtraction *(3, 11)*.

Quantities *(pages 7, 8, 9, 10, 14, 15, 24, 25, 26, 27)*

Children can learn the various terms such as mass and temperature *(9, 24)*. Simple projects help them to understand these measurements *(7, 8, 10, 25, 26, 27)*. Children also learn to tell the time *(14)*. Simple fractions are shown in practical contexts *(15)*.

Space *(pages 5, 6, 12, 13, 20, 21, 22)*

Children learn about simple geometric shapes and discover their names *(5, 6, 20, 21, 22)*. Making patterns with shapes helps to further their understanding of them *(23)* and they begin to have an understanding of area *(12, 13)*.

Mechanisms *(pages 16, 17)*

Science and mathematics are closely linked studies. Simple mechanisms which illustrate force, such as wheels, pulleys and levers, are now included in most maths courses.

Pictorial representation *(page 19)*

Pictorial representation by graphs of various kinds is one way for children to learn analysis, and it enables them to store information conveniently as well as to interpret it.